Collins · *do brilliantly !*

Instant**Facts**

English

A-Z of **essential facts** and definitions

Graham King

William Collins' dream of knowledge for all began with the publication of his first book in 1819. A self-educated mill worker, he not only enriched millions of lives, but also founded a flourishing publishing house. Today, staying true to this spirit, Collins books are packed with inspiration, innovation and practical expertise. They place you at the centre of a world of possibility and give you exactly what you need to explore it.

Collins. Do more.

Published by Collins
An imprint of HarperCollins*Publishers*
77 – 85 Fulham Palace Road
Hammersmith
London
W6 8JB

Browse the complete Collins catalogue at

www.collinseducation.com
© HarperCollins*Publishers* Limited 2005

10 9 8 7 6 5 4 3 2 1

ISBN 0 00 720552 X

British Library Cataloguing in Publication Data
A catalogue record for this publication is available from the British Library

Edited and Project Managed by Marie Insall
Production by Katie Butler
Designed by Sally Boothroyd
Printed and bound by Printing Express, Hong Kong

You might also like to visit
www.harpercollins.co.uk
The book lover's website

Introduction

Instant Facts English is one of a series of A-Z subject reference dictionaries of the key terms and concepts used in the most important school subjects. With its alphabetical arrangement, the book is designed for quick reference to explain the meaning of words used in the subject and so provides a companion both to course work and during revision.

Highlighted words in an entry identify key terms which are explained in greater detail in entries of their own; examples within entries are shown in *italic*.

Other titles in the *Instant Facts* series include:
Modern World History
Biology
Science
Physics
Geography
Maths
Chemistry

A

a- A prefix that forms adjectives which have *not, without,* or *opposite* in their meaning. For example, *atypical* behaviour is not typical of someone.

abbreviation The shortened or contracted form of a word, name or phrase. For example, *A & E* is the abbreviation of Accident and Emergency.

-ability and **-ibility** Suffixes that replace *-able* and *-ible* at the end of adjectives to form nouns which refer to a particular state or quality. For example, *reliability* is the state or quality of being reliable.

-able A suffix that forms adjectives which indicate what someone or something can have done to them. For example, if something is *readable*, it can be read.

abstract noun A noun used to refer to a quality, idea, feeling, or experience, rather than a physical object: *existence, size, reason, joy.*

active voice The active voice and the passive voice are two different ways of presenting information in a sentence. When a sentence is written in the active voice, the subject of the verb is doing the action.

Would you rather do something, or have something done to you? With the first choice, you are in control (active); in the second you are the subject of somebody's whim (passive).

Active *The favourite won the 3.30 hurdle event.*
Her boyfriend bought the ring.

Passive *The 3.30 hurdle event was won by the favourite.*
The ring was bought by her boyfriend.

It's easy to see why one kind of sentence is called active and the other passive; active sentences are direct and personal and seem more interesting, while passive sentences tend to be detached and impersonal by comparison.

adjective An adjective is a word that tells you something about a noun. They are sometimes called 'describing words' and have many uses:

Adjectives may **indicate how many of a person or thing there are**:
three men
some fish

Adjectives may **describe feelings or qualities**:
a *happy* child
a *strange* girl

Adjectives may **describe size, age, temperature, or measurement**:
a *large* envelope
an *old* jacket

Adjectives may **indicate colour**:
red socks
dark hair

Adjectives may **indicate nationality or origin**:
my *Indian* cousin
a *northern* accent

Adjectives may **indicate the material from which something is made**:
a *wooden* box
denim trousers

adjunct Another name for adverbial.

adverb An adverb gives more information about *when, how, where* or
in what circumstances something happens:

Adverbs of manner answer the question *"how?"*:
She runs *quickly*.
She sings *badly*.

Adverbs of place answer the question *"where?"*:
We travelled *northwards*.
I live *here*.

Adverbs of time answer the question *"when?"*:
You must stop *immediately*.
I arrived *yesterday*.

Adverbs of degree answer the question *"to what extent?"*:
I *really* hope you will stay.
I play golf fairly *often*.

Adverbs of frequency answer the question *"how often?"*:
We *sometimes* meet for lunch.
You *never* answer my questions.

Sometimes adverbs can refer to the whole sentence rather than just the verb:
Fortunately, she was not badly hurt.

An Adverb defines and modifies verbs, adjectives and other adverbs:

Modifying a verb He trudged *wearily* along the road.
How did he walk along the road?

Modifying an adjective She's an *exceedingly* lucky girl.
To *what extent* is she lucky?

Modifying another adverb The engine turned over *very* smoothly.
How smoothly did it turn over?

Always keep adverbs such as *nearly, only, even, quite, just,* etc, as near as possible to the words they're meant to modify. For example, '*She just went to the store to buy some jeans*' appears to mean that, only a short while ago, she went to the store to buy some jeans. But what the statement was intended to convey was '*She went to the store just to buy some jeans*'.

adverbial An adverb, or an adverb phrase, prepositional phrase, or noun group which does the same job as an adverb, giving more information about *when, how, where,* or *in what* circumstances something happens: *then, very quickly, in the street, the next day.*

aero- A prefix that forms words, especially nouns, that refer to things or activities connected with air or movement through the air. For example, an *aeroplane* is a vehicle which flies through the air.

affirmative A clause or sentence in the affirmative is one which does not contain a negative word such as *not* and which is not a question.

-al A suffix that forms adjectives which indicate what something is connected with. For example, *environmental* problems are problems connected with the environment.

alliteration The use of the same consonant or vowel in words adjacent or near one another. For example, *Peter Piper picked a peck of pickled peppers.*

-ally A suffix that is added to adjectives ending in *-ic* to form adverbs which indicate how something is done or what something relates to. For example, if something is done *enthusiastically*, it is done in an enthusiastic way.

-ance, -ence, -ancy and **-ency** Suffixes that form nouns which refer to a particular action, state, or quality. For example, *brilliance* is the state or quality of being brilliant, and *reappearance* is the action of reappearing.

-ancy See -ance.

anti- A prefix that forms nouns and adjectives which refer to some sort of opposition. For example, an *anti-government* demonstration is a demonstration against the government.

apostrophe There are two kinds of apostrophe. One kind indicates the possession of something; the other kind indicates a contraction or abbreviation – a letter or letters left out of a word:

Possessive apostrophe
Did you know *Jack's* car is a write-off?
I heard that *Jack's* kids have the flu.

Contraction apostrophe
Did you know that *Jack's* had a bad accident?
I heard that *Jack'll* be out tomorrow.

In the first two examples the apostrophes tell us that the car and the kids belong to Jack; they are possessive apostrophes. In the second pair of examples the apostrophes tell us that something is left out: that *Jack's* is a shortened version of *Jack is*, and that *Jack'll* is a shortened version of *Jack will*; they are contraction apostrophes.

Possessive apostrophes
If we wish to indicate that something belongs to somebody we use the possessive apostrophe:
Joyce's house, Michael's mountain bike, the girl's tunic, his uncle's car, her grandfather's clock.

Possession, ownership or association can also apply to things: *a good day's work, the company's policy, the tree's branches, the door's hinges.*

And the same goes for certain plural nouns:
men's trousers, children's toys, mice's tails, people's charter.

The problem is that adding possessive apostrophes to words and names, such as *boss, surplus, Thomas*, and to plurals, such as *cats, hours* and *friends*, is not such a straightforward business. Here are some examples:

Words and names ending with -*s* possessive form
the boss → *the boss's temper*
Thomas → *Thomas's recent illness*
mistress → *a mistress's secrets*
Charles Dickens → *Dicken's novels*

Now see what happens when plural nouns that end with -*s* become possessive:

Plural words ending with -*s* possessive form
Tamar's parents → *Tamar's parents' caravan*
her friends → *her friends' parties*
the members → *the members' privileges*
our employees →*our employees' bonuses*
the girls → *the girls' classroom*

For singular ownership we simply add -*s*, but for plural or shared ownership we add the apostrophe after the -*s*'. The system enables us to distinguish the different meanings. When we read:
The opera star heard the girl's singing
we are being told that the star listened to only one girl singing, whereas
The opera star heard the girls' singing
tells us (if we've learned the rules!) that the diva is listening to many girls singing.

In some cases, especially with names, we have choices, according to taste. We can add the final -*s* (*Tom Jones's songs, Prince Charles's opinions*) or drop it (*Wales' ruggedness, Dickens' character*), or observe tradition (*Queens' College, Cambridge; Queen's College, Oxford*).

However, beware of adjectives that look like possessives, such as games mistress, that require no apostrophe. And watch out for units of time, such as *a day's work, a minute's delay and six months' salary* in complex sentences such as these:
I'm taking a three weeks holiday in three weeks' time.
An hour's delay or two hours' delay – I wish the airline would tell us the facts.

In the first example, the first *three weeks* is an adjective phrase modifying the noun *holiday*. The second *three weeks'* has a possessive apostrophe to indicate that they are attached to the time that will elapse before the holiday is taken. In the second sentence both apostrophes are possessive: the first attached to the singular hour – *hour's*, and the second to the plural hours – *hours'*.

Pronouns can also be perplexing. Some have possessive apostrophes and some do not:

Contraction Apostrophes
Pronouns with apostrophes *one's problems, anyone's idea, someone's shoes, one another's responsibilities, nobody's fault, anybody's luggage, each other's possessions*
Pronouns without apostrophes *his, hers, its, ours, yours, theirs*

One of the most frequent errors is the use of *it's* for the possessive form of *it*. This is wrong, of course: *it's* is the accepted contraction for *it is* or *it has*. For the record:

Possession
The newspaper claimed its punctuation record was unmatched by any of its rivals.

Contraction
It's (It is) a fact that the punctuation record of the newspaper isn't (is not) so clever after all.

Also for the record is this list of most of the accepted contractions:

aren't	are not	she'll	she will, she shall
can't	cannot, can not	she's	she is, she has
couldn't	could not	there's	there is, there has
hasn't	has not	they'll	they will, they shall
haven't	have not	they're	they are
he'll	he will, he shall	they've	they have
he's	he is, he has	we'll	we will, we shall
I'd	I would, I had	weren't	were not
I'm	I am	who's	who is, who has
it's	it is, it has	won't	will not
I've	I have	wouldn't	would not
let's	let us	you'll	you will, you shall
ma'am	madam	you're	you are
mustn't	must not	you've	you have

There are many more idiomatic contractions: *sweet'n'lo, 'alf a mo', finger lickin', Ah'm talkin' to yuh, rock'n'roll*, and so forth. Some antique contractions survive: *o'er* (over), *ne'er* (never) and *e'en* (even). But quite a few common words formerly carrying contraction apostrophes ('cello, 'flu, 'phone, 'til, standing for violoncello, influenza, *telephone* and *until*) are now accepted without them.

One final apostrophic tip: *who's* is short for *who is* or *who has*; *whose* indicates possession: *whose wallet is this?*

article The word *a* is known as the indefinite article. You use it before a singular noun to refer to any example of that noun, or to avoid being specific about which example you mean:
a school
a woman

The word *an* is used instead of *a* when a word begins with a vowel sound:
an elephant
an umpire

The word *an* is also used instead of *a* when words sound as though they begin with a vowel:
an hour
an honour

The word *a* is used instead of *an* when words that begin with a vowel sound as though they begin with a consonant:
a union
a European

assonance The use of the same vowel sound with different consonants or the same consonant with different vowels, as in a line of verse. Examples are *time* and *light*, or *mystery* and *mastery*.

asterisk A star-shaped character (*) used in writing to indicate a cross-reference to a footnote or an omission.

astro- A prefix that is used to form words which refer to things relating to the stars or to outer space. For example, an *astronaut* is a person who travels in space.

-ation, -ication, -sion and **-tion** Suffixes that form nouns which refer to a state or process, or to an instance of that process. For example, the *protection* of the environment is the process of protecting it.

auto- A prefix that forms words which refer to someone doing something *to, for,* or *about* themselves. For example, your *autobiography* is an account of your life, which you write yourself.

auxiliary Another name for auxiliary verb.

auxiliary verb There are two kinds of auxiliary verb: the three primary auxiliaries (*be, do, has*) which often double as main verbs; and what are known as modal auxiliaries (*can/could, may/might, must, shall/should, will/would*) which form verb phrases which enable us to express an amazing range of meanings: whether or not something is possible; making demands; giving permission; deducing or predicting some event etc. And, by following such verb phrases by negatives (*not, never*) we can express an equal range of opposite meanings. There are other such things as fringe modals that contribute other possibilities: *I ought/ought not to go. Dare I go? I used to go. I had better/better not go. I would rather/rather not to. Need I go?...*etc.

B

base form The form of a verb without any endings added to it, which is used in the *to* infinitive and for the imperative: *walk, go, have, be*. The base form is the form you look up in a dictionary.

be The verb *to be* has a lot of unusual forms, and does not follow the usual rules.

The main form is *be*. This is used with an auxiliary verb to make compound tenses, and after the preposition *to*:
She will *be* five years old in April.

The verb forms *am, are*, and *is* are used to talk about the present time. *Am* is used for the first person singular; *are* is used for the second person and for all plural forms; *is* is used for the third person singular:
I *am* exhausted.
You *are* very welcome.
Haresh *is* always cheerful.
They *are* a pair of rascals.

The present participle is *being*. This form is used with an auxiliary verb to make compound tenses:
Matthew *was being* very helpful.

The verb forms *was* and *were* talk about past time. *Was* is used for the first and third person singular; *were* is used for the second person and for all plural forms:
I *was* exhausted.
You *were* very welcome.
Robbie *was* always cheerful.
They *were* a pair of rascals.

The past participle is *been*. This form is used with an auxiliary verb to make compound tenses:
I shall *have been* here five years in April.
Robbie *has been* polite at all times.

be- A prefix that can be added to a noun followed by an *-ed* suffix to form an adjective that indicates that a person is covered with or wearing the thing named. For example, a person who is *bespectacled* is wearing spectacles.

bi- A prefix that forms nouns and adjectives which have two as part of their meaning. For example, if someone is *bilingual*, they speak two languages. It also forms adjectives and adverbs which refer to something happening twice in a period of time, or once in two consecutive periods of time. For example, a *bimonthly* event happens twice a month, or once every two months.

bio- A prefix that is used at the beginning of nouns and adjectives that refer to life or to the study of living things. For example, a *biography* is a book about someone's life.

bracket See parenthesis or square brackets.

bullet point It has found increasing favour, perhaps because:
- It enables us to summarise clearly a series of facts or conclusions.
- It sends a signal to the eye that 'here are the essentials'.
- It encourages writers to be brief: to use words and phrases rather than long sentences.
- It captures readers who are too lazy or too harassed to read solid texts.

C

capitalisation Capital letters are a form of punctuation in that they help guide the eye and mind through a text. Try reading this:

on sunday, april 7, easter day, after having been at st paul's cathedral, i came to dr johnson, according to my usual custom. johnson and i supt at the crown and anchor tavern, in company with sir joshua reynolds, mr langton, mr [william] nairne, now one of the scotch judges, with the title of lord dunsinan, and my very worthy friend, sir william forbes, of pitsligo.

It's a paragraph shorn of capital letters. It's readable, with some effort, but how much easier would the eye glide through it were it sign-posted with capitals at the start of each sentence, proper name and the abbreviation Mr! Capitals are used at the beginning of sentences, after full stops, and for the first word in direct speech:

Correct *Sentences begin with capitals. And they follow full stops.*

Wrong *They do not follow commas, Nor do they follow semicolons or colons; But they do follow exclamation and question marks.*

Correct *He told us, 'Always use a capital when quoting direct speech.'*

Wrong *He told us, 'always use a capital when quoting direct speech.'*

Guide to Capitalisation

Aircraft Concorde, Airbus, Boeing 747, etc.

Armed forces *British Army, Italian Navy, Brazilian Air Force,* but *navy, air force. Ranks are capitalised: Sergeant, Admiral, Lieutenant,* etc.

The calendar *Monday, March, Good Friday, the Millennium Dome* but *the new millennium.*

Compass points *northwest, south-southwest, but mysterious East, deep South, frozen North.*

Days *Christmas Day, New Year's Day, Derby Day.*

The Deity *God, Father, Almighty, Holy Ghost, Jesus Christ;* also *Bible, New Testament, Book of Common Prayer, Koran, Talmud,* etc; and religions (*Judaism, Baptists, B'nai B'rith*). *Hades,* but *heaven and hell.*

Diplomatic *Nicaraguan embassy* (embassy is lower case).

Dog breeds *Labrador, Afghan hound, Scotch terrier*, etc, but *rottweiler, lurcher, bulldog*, etc, lower case (check the dictionary as capitalisation is inconsistent).

Exclamations *Oh! Ahrrgh! Wow!*

First person pronoun *I told them that I was leaving.*

Flora and fauna *Arab horse, Shetland pony, Montague's harrier* but *hen harrier* (capitals where a proper name is involved). Plants are lower case, but with scientific names, orders, classes, families and genuses are capitalised; species and varieties are lower case: *Agaricus bisporus.*

Geographical *The West, the East, the Orient, Northern Hemisphere, Third World, British Commonwealth, the Gulf, the Midlands, South-East Asia.*

Headlines With capital and lower-case headlines, capitalise nouns, pronouns, verbs and words of four or more letters. Generally, capitalise *No, Not, Off, Out, So, Up* but not *a, and, as, at, but, by, for, if, in, of, on, the, to* except when they begin headlines. Capitalise both parts of hyphenated compounds: *Sit-In, Cease-Fire, Post-War.*

Heavenly bodies Mars, Venus, Uranus, Ursa Major, Halley's Comet.

History *Cambrian Era, Middle Ages, Elizabethan, the Depression, Renaissance, Year of the Rat.*

Law and lords *Lord Chancellor, Lord Privy Seal, Queen's Counsel.*

Local government *council*, but *Kent County Council, Enfield Borough Council, Lord Mayor of Manchester.*

Member of Parliament lower case, except when abbreviated: *MP.*

Nations, Nationalities *Venezuela, Alaska, Brits, Estonians, Sudanese. Indian ink, Indian file, Indian clubs, but indian summer; French polish, French stick, French kiss, French letter* but *french window; Chinese*, but *chinaware; Turkish bath, Turkish delight.*

Personification *The family gods were Hope and Charity.*

Political parties *Tory, Conservative Party, Labour Party, Liberal terms Democrats, Communist Party*, but *communist, Thatcherism, Leninist, Luddites, Marxist, Gaullist*, etc.

Popes *The Pope*, but *popes, Pope Paul, Pope John*, etc.

Proper names Names of people (*Tony Blair, Spice Girls*); places (*Europe, Mt Everest*); titles (*Pride and Prejudice, Ten O'Clock News*); epithets (*Iron Duke, Iron Lady*); nicknam*es (Elvis 'The King' Presley, Winston 'The Buuldog' Churchill*)

Races *Aztecs, Shawnees, Aboriginals, Asiatics.*

Religion *Sister Wendy, Mother Teresa, Archbishop of Canterbury, Catholics, Jew, Jewish, Semitic, anti-Semitism, Protestants.*

Royalty *The Queen, Duke of Edinburgh, Prince of Wales, Queen Mother, Princess Anne, the Crown.*

Rulers *Her Majesty's Government, House of Commons, Secretary of State, Chancellor of the Exchequer; Prime Minister* (PM when abbreviated).

Satirised references *In Crowd, Heavy Brigade, She Who Must Be Obeyed, Bright Young Things, Her Indoors.*

Scouts *Scouts, Guides, Cubs.*

Seasons *spring, summer, autumn, winter* (all lower case).

Street names *road, avenue, crescent, square*, etc, but *Highfield Road, Spring Avenue, Eagle Crescent, Sloane Square*, etc.

Titles *Sir Thomas More, Lord Asquith, Mr and Mrs, Dr,* etc.

Trade names, marks *Hoover, Peugeot, Kentucky Fried Chicken, Gillette, Xerox,* etc.

Van When writing Dutch names van is lower case when part of the full name (*Hans van Meegeren, Vincent van Gogh*) but capitalised when used only with the surname (*Van Gogh, Van Dyke*).

von In Germanic names, *von* is always lower case.

World War Capitalise, as in *World War I, World War II.* The usage First World War or Second World War is sometimes preferred.

cardinal number A number used in counting: *one, seven, nineteen.*

clause A clause is a unit of related words, which contains a subject and other words, always including a verb, which gives us information about the subject:
The patient stopped breathing, so I shouted for the nurse.

In this example, *The patient stopped breathing* is a main clause of the sentence, because it can stand alone. In fact, if you put a full stop after *breathing* it becomes a legitimate sentence. But *I shouted for the nurse* is also a compound sentence consisting of two main clauses coordinated by the adverb *so* – here used as a conjunction:

main clause	coordinator	main clause
The patient stopped breathing	*so*	*I shouted for the nurse.*

Now let's construct a sentence in a different way – this time with a main clause and a subordinate clause:
This is the patient who stopped breathing.

You can pick the main clause because it can stand on its own: *This is the patient.* The rest of the sentence consists of *who stopped breathing*, which is the subordinate clause because it can't stand on its own.

main clause	subordinate clause
This is the patient	*who stopped breathing.*

You can add more information to a subordinate clause, but regardless of how much extra information you pile on it remains a subordinate clause because it is always subordinate to the main clause, serving only to influence the word *patient*:

main clause	subordinate clause
This is the patient	*who, when I visited the hospital yesterday, stopped breathing for several minutes.*

Subordinate clauses have the ability to function as nouns, adjectives and adverbs:

Noun clause – where the clause acts as a noun.
She told him *what she thought.*

Adjectival clause – where the clause acts as an adjective.
This is the door *that won't close properly.*

Adverbial clause – where the clause acts as an adverb.
You should go there *before the shops open.*

Adjectival clauses are introduced by the relative pronouns *that* and *which*. These and *who, where, whose, what* and *as* are typically used for this purpose, which is why adjectival clauses are sometimes referred to as relative clauses.

Functioning as adverbs, the adverbial clauses give information about time, place and purpose. The sentence *You should go there before the shops open* could be saying *You should go there* [*now, soon, quickly*] – all of which are adverbs. In this case, however, the adverbial clause *before the shops open* may have been chosen over a simple adverb as being more informative.

cliché A word or expression that has lost much of its force through overexposure, for example, *put your money where your mouth is*.

co- A **prefix** that forms verbs and nouns which refer to people sharing things or doing things together. For example, if two people *co-write* a book, they write it together. The *co-author* of a book is one of the people who has written it.

collective noun A noun that identifies groups of things, people, animals and ideas: *audience, council, staff, team, enemy, collection, herd, quantity.* The effect of a collective noun is to create a singular entity which, although many creatures (bees in a *swarm*), people (members of a *jury*) or objects (a number of *entries*) are involved, should be treated as a singular noun:
The *army* is outside the city gates.
Will *this* class please behave itself?
The *management* has refused to meet us.

Sometimes, however, a collective noun takes the singular or plural form according to context:
A vast *number* of crimes *is/are* never reported at all.
The *majority is/are* in favour of the merger.

It is important that once you are committed to a singular or plural verb, you stick to it:

Not   The Tilner Committee *has* a week in which to announce *their* findings.

But   The Tilner Committee *has* a week in which to announce *its* findings.

Or   The Tilner Committee *have* a week in which to announce *their* findings.

colloquialism An informal word or phrase used especially in conversation. For example, *give us a break.*

colon The colon acts as a pointing finger, as if to warn the reader about a statement ahead: Wait for it ... here it comes! It has a range of functions:

To introduce a list
This is probably how colons are most commonly used:
Detective Stevens entered and took it all in: the body, the still smouldering mattress, the cigarette butts on the floor.

To present a conclusion
There was one very obvious reason for Ernest's failure to keep the job: his right hand never knew what his left was doing.

To present an explanation or example
There are three reasons why Lainston House near Winchester is an outstanding restaurant: excellent cuisine, beautifully restored interiors, and super-attentive staff.

To introduce a quotation or indirect speech
Gradually, one by one, the words came back to me: 'And we forget because we must and not because we will.'
'The Mayor strode to the platform, opened his notes and glared at the assembly: 'You have not come here for nothing,' he growled.

As a substitute for a conjunction
In this example, the writer preferred the punchier colon to a choice of conjunctions such as *and* or *but*:
Rodriguez felled him with a dazzling left hook that came out of nowhere: Hayman did not get up.

To introduce questions
The essential issue is simply this: did she or did she not die in the stable block?

To introduce subtitles
Gilbert White: Observer in God's Little Acre.
Men at War: An Introduction to Chess.

To link contrasting statements
In this role the colon shares with the semicolon the ability to administer surprise and shock. The choice is a matter of taste:

Her love affair with her son's school, its history, its achievements, its famous alumni and its crumbling charm would have endured for ever but for one minor consideration: the £12,000 yearly fees.

Other sundry uses
If you ever read a stageplay, you'll often find it laid out something like this:
GEORGE: *You've said enough –*
ANNA: *I haven't even started!*
GEORGE: *Enough! D'you hear me!*

Then there is the 'biblical' colon, separating chapter and verse (Ecclesiastes 3:12); the mathematical colon used to express ratios *(Male athletes outnumber females by 3:2)*; and the time colon (The train departs at 12:45).

It's worth remembering that: the difference between a colon and a semicolon is not a difference in weight or force; the two marks are mostly used for quite different purposes. Except in the case of introducing subtitles (see above), a colon is not followed by a capital letter unless the word is a proper noun: *Emma, Ford Motor Co*, etc. Don't use colons where they are not needed, as in: *The man was amazing and was able to play: the piano, violin, double bass, trombone, clarinet, harp and drums.* The colon here is clearly redundant.

comma The comma is the most flexible and most versatile of all the punctuation marks. The comma's broad function is to separate words, phrases and clauses in a sentence to help it to be understood – to divide a sentence into easily assimilated bite-sized pieces. That is the basic function of the comma, but there are many others:

Setting apart names and persons
Are you meeting him tomorrow, John?
Listen, Joyce, I've had enough.
And that, ladies and gentlemen, is that.

Itemising words
Please place all towels, costumes, clothing and valuables in the lockers provided.

Itemising word groups
Please place any articles of clothing, swimming and sporting equipment, personal belongings, but not money and jewellery, in the lockers.

Enclosing additional thoughts or qualifications
The occasion was, on the whole, conducted with considerable dignity.

Qualifications
The judges thought it was, arguably, one of his finest novels.

Setting apart
Look, I've had enough!

Interjections
Blimey, isn't the beach crowded!

Before direct speech
Gul turned abruptly and said, 'If that's the way you feel, then go home!

Introducing questions
You'll be going soon, won't you?
She's marrying James tomorrow, isn't she?

Emphasising points of view
Naturally, I'll look after the car.
Of course, she fully deserves it.

Setting off comparative or contrasting statements
The taller they are, the farther they fall.
The more he said he adored Maisie, the less she cared.

Reinforcing statements
She's ill because she won't eat, that's why!
It'll come right in the end, I'm sure.

After introductory words
Chips, which are far from fat-free, pose a problem for dieters.

command Commands are used to give orders, instructions, or warnings by putting the verb at the start of the sentence. The verb is used in its **imperative** form, which is the basic form without any endings added: *Come over here.*

Commands do not need a subject because people who are being told to do something already know who they are. So commands may consist of a single verb:
Stop!

The negative form of a command is introduced by *do not* or *don't*:
Don't put that on the table.

Commands often end with an exclamation mark rather than a full stop, especially if they express urgency:
Run for your life!

comparative There are three forms of adjectives: the basic positive, the comparative, and the superlative. The comparative form of an adjective is used to make comparisons between people, things, or states.

The comparative form is usually made by adding the ending *-er* to the positive form of the adjective. If the second part of the comparison is mentioned it follows *than*. It shows that something possesses a quality to a greater extent than the thing it is being compared with:
Matthew is *taller than* Anna.

You can also make comparisons by using the words *more* or *less* with the positive (not the comparative) form of the adjective:
Matthew is *more energetic* than Robbie.

Irregular Comparative Forms
When the comparative and superlative of an adjective are not formed in the regular way, the irregular forms of the adjective are shown in the dictionary after the main entry.

Many adjectives – especially ones that have more than one syllable and do not end in *-y* – do not have separate spelling forms for the comparative and superlative. For these adjectives comparisons must be made using *more, less, most, and least*:
beautiful → more beautiful → most beautiful
boring → less boring → least boring

complement A noun group or adjective, which comes after a link verb such as *be*, and gives more information about the subject of the clause:
She is a teacher... she is tired.

complex sentence A sentence that consists of a main clause and a subordinate clause, which would not make sense alone.

compound noun A word formed from two existing words: *mother-in-law, grass-roots etc.*

compound sentence A sentence that consists of two main clauses, joined by a conjunction such as *and, but, or*. Each clause is of equal importance and gives information of equal value.

conditional clause A subordinate clause, usually starting with *if* or *unless*, which is used to talk about possible situations and their results:
They would be rich *if they had taken my advice.*
We'll go to the park, *unless it rains.*

conjunction A conjunction is a word that joins two words or two parts of a sentence together. Conjunctions are sometimes called "joining words".

Coordinating conjunctions join items of equal importance:
I ordered fish *and* chips.

Contrasting conjunctions are a type of coordinating conjunction which are used to join opposites or contrasting items:
He was not walking *but* running.

Correlative conjunctions are pairs of conjunctions, such as *either ... or,* or *both ... and,* each of which introduces a separate item in the sentence:
She speaks *both* French *and* German.
You can drink *either* tea *or* coffee.

Subordinating conjunctions join additional items to the main part of the sentence:
He was happy *because* he had finished his work.
I will come *if* I have time.

continuous tense A tense which contains a form of the verb *be* and a present participle:
She *was* laughing.
They *had been* playing badminton.

contraction See apostrophe.

contrast clause A subordinate clause, usually introduced by *although* or *in spite of the fact that*, which contrasts with a main clause:
Although I like her, I find her hard to talk to.

countable noun Another name for count noun.

counter- A prefix that forms words which refer to actions or activities that oppose another action or activity. For example, a *counter-measure* is an action you take to weaken the effect of another action or situation.

count noun A noun which has both singular and plural forms: *dog/dogs, foot/feet lemon/lemons.*

-cy A suffix that forms nouns which refer to a particular state or quality. For example, *accuracy* is the state or quality of being accurate.

D

dash The dash marks an abrupt change in the flow of a sentence and has many uses:

Linking device
Mrs Sims had four daughters – Poppy, Iris, Pansy and Petal.

As a pause
Everyone expected the poet to be controversial – but not to the extent of swearing at the chairwoman and falling off the stage.

Cueing a surprise
The adhesive gave way, the beard came adrift and Santa Claus was revealed as – Aunt Clara!

Noting an exception
I get up at 6 a.m. every day – during the week.

Indicating hesitation
There will be, of course, er- a small charge, because – well, er -.

Separating lists
She assembled all the ingredients – flour, sugar, eggs, salt, lard and raisins – and started on the pudding.

Afterthoughts
They babbled on, delighted at sighting the rare parakeet – I didn't see so much as a feather.

de- A **prefix** added to some verbs to make verbs which mean the opposite. For example, to *deactivate* a mechanism means to switch it off so that it cannot work.

defining relative clause A relative clause which identifies the person or thing that is being talked about:
The lady *who lives next door.*
I wrote down *everything that she said.*

definite article The determiner *the*.

demi- A prefix used at the beginning of some words to refer to something equivalent to half of the object or amount indicated by the rest of the word. For example, a *demigod* is a god which is half god and half human.

demonstrative One of the words *this, that, these,* and *those: this house.*

determiner One of a group of words including *the, a, some,* and *my,* which are used at the beginning of a noun group.

direct object A noun group referring to the person or thing affected by an action, in a clause with a verb in the active voice:
She wrote her *name.*
I shut *the windows.*

direct speech The actual words spoken by someone.

dis- A prefix that can be added to some words to form words which have the opposite meaning. For example, if someone is *dishonest*, they are not honest.

E

e- A prefix that is used to form words that indicate that something happens on or uses the Internet. *E-* is an abbreviation for *electronic*. For example, *e-business* is the buying, selling, and ordering of goods and services using the Internet.

eco- A prefix that forms nouns and adjectives which refer to something related to the environment. For example, *eco-friendly* products do not harm the environment.

-ed The suffix that is added to verbs to make the past tense and past participle. Past participles formed are often used as adjectives which indicate that something has been affected in some way. For example, *cooked food* is food that has been cooked.

ellipsis This line of dots indicates missing matter, which may consist of a single word or matter considered to be non-essential:
Yesterday the shares stood at just over £4.65, which if you believe last night's closing statement ... at that price the company is valued at almost £1.6 billion.

or an implied quotation or phrase that the reader is expected to know:
So then she bought contact lenses: you know, men don't make passes ... And she really believes that, too!

or indicating an unfinished thought:
The troubling question was, would Mrs Benedict sue, or ...

or indicating a time lapse:
Kimball crashed to the floor with eye-wincing force ... only later, much later, in the darkness, did he realise he was a marked man.

or indicating disjointed speech:
She paced the room. 'I don't know ... every way I look at it ... what would you do?' She drew deeply on the cigarette. 'I mean, surely he wouldn't do this to me ... or would he?'

em- The prefix that is a form of *en-* that is used before *b-, m-* and *p-*. See en-.

en- The prefix that is added to words to form verbs that describe the process of putting someone into a particular state, condition or place, or to form adjectives and nouns that describe that process or those states and conditions. For example, if you *endanger* someone or something, you put them in a situation where they might be harmed or destroyed.

-ence See -ance.

-ency See -ance.

enjambement The running over of text from one line of verse into the next.

-er and **-or** Suffixes which form nouns which refer to a person who performs a particular action, often because it is their job. For example, a *teacher* is someone who teaches. *-er* and *-or* also form nouns which refer to tools and machines that form a particular action. For example, a *mixer* is a machine that mixes things. The *-er* suffixes are also added to many short adjectives to form comparatives. For example, the comparative of *nice* is *nicer* and the comparative of *happy* is *happier*. You also add it to some adverbs that do not end in *-ly*. For example, the comparative of *soon* is *sooner*.

ergative verb a verb which is both transitive and intransitive in the same meaning. The object of the transitive use is the subject of the intransitive use: *He boiled a kettle... The kettle boiled.*

-est A suffix that is added to many short adjectives to form superlatives. For example, the superlative of *nice* is *nicest*, and the superlative of *happy* is *happiest*. You also add it to some adverbs that do not end in *-ly*. For example, the superlative of *soon* is *soonest*.

euphemism An inoffensive word or phrase substituted for one considered offensive or hurtful. For example, a deaf person is often described as *hard of hearing*.

euro- A prefix that is used to form words that describe or refer to something which is connected with Europe or with the European Union. For example, If you describe something as *Eurocentric*, you disapprove of it because it focuses on Europe and the needs of European people, often with the result that people in other parts of the world suffer in some way.

ex- A prefix that forms words which refer to people who are no longer a particular thing. For example, an *ex-policeman* is someone who is no longer a policeman.

exclamation mark The exclamation mark is used after emphatic expressions and exclamations:
I can't believe it!

It's hard to imagine the following examples conveying anything like the same force and feeling without the exclamation mark:
Shut up! What a mess!

Literature would undoubtedly be the poorer without them. Good writers aren't afraid of exclamation marks and use them for a number of functions:

Conveying anger *You're out of your mind!*

Scorn/disgust *You must be joking!*

Indicating sarcasm *Thanks a lot!*

Reverse meaning *That's just lovely, that is!*

Conveying an ironic tone *You're not so smart! And you said we wouldn't win!*

Commanding *Come here! Right now! Get lost! And don't come back!*

The exclamation mark can lose its effect if used too much. After a sentence expressing mild excitement or humour, it is better to use a full stop:
It is a beautiful day.

extra- A prefix that forms adjectives which refer to something being outside or beyond something else. For example, Britain's *extra-European commitments* are its commitments outside of Europe. It also forms adjectives which refer to something having a large amount of a particular quality. For example, if something is *extra-strong*, it is very strong.

F

feminine Feminine nouns denote female people and animals:
The *girl* put on her coat.
It is customary to refer to countries and vehicles as if they were feminine:
The ship came into view, her sails swelling in the breeze.

Common nouns may be either masculine or feminine. Other words in the
sentence may tell us if they are male or female:
The doctor parked *his* car.
The doctor parked *her* car.

figurative A word or expression that is used with a more abstract or
imaginative meaning than its ordinary one.

first person See person.

-fold A suffix that combines with numbers to form adverbs which say
how much an amount has increased by. For example, if an amount
increases *fourfold*, it is four times greater than it was originally.

-ful A suffix that forms nouns which refer to the amount of a substance
that something contains or can contain. For example, a *handful* of sand is
the amount of sand that you can hold in your hand.

future tense See tense.

full stop The full stop is used like a knife to cut off a sentence at the
required length. The rule is that simple: where you place your stop is up to
you, but generally it is at the point where a thought is complete. When you
are about to embark on another thought, that's the time to think about a
full stop. Master this principle and you can then move on to using full
stops stylistically, for emphasis.

Full stops control the length of your sentences, so remember:

• Try to keep sentences variable in length, but generally short.

• Using long sentences doesn't necessarily make you a better writer.

• Consider the use of other punctuation marks, in addition to full stops.

future There is no simple future tense in English. To talk about an event that will happen in the future, we usually use compound tenses.

The auxiliary verbs will and shall are used before the basic form of the verb to show that an action will happen:
His father *will* cook the dinner.
I *shall* cook the dinner.

You can also talk about the future by putting the verbs *will have* or *shall have* before the verb, and adding the ending -*ed*. This form shows that an action will be completed in the future:
His father *will have cooked* the dinner.
I *shall have cooked* the dinner.

You can also talk about the future by using the phrase *be about to* or *be going to* in front of the dictionary form of the verb. This shows that the action will take place very soon:
He *is about to* cook the dinner.
I *am going to* cook the dinner.

You can sometimes use a form of the present tense to talk about future events, but only if the sentence contains a clear reference to the future:
His father *is cooking* the dinner *tonight*.
The plane *leaves* at *three o'clock*.

G

gender When we talk about the gender of a noun, we mean whether it is referred to as *he, she,* or *it*. There are three genders: *masculine* (things referred to as *he*), *feminine* (things referred to as *she*), and *neuter* (things referred to as *it*).

Masculine nouns refer to male people and animals:
The *boy* put on *his* coat.

Feminine nouns denote female people and animals:
The *girl* put on *her* coat.

It is customary to refer to countries and vehicles as if they were feminine.
The *ship* came into view, her *sails* swelling in the breeze.

Neuter nouns refer to inanimate objects and abstract ideas:
The *kettle* will switch *itself* off.

Common nouns may be either masculine or feminine. Other words in the sentence may tell us if they are male or female:
The *doctor* parked *his* car.
The *doctor* parked *her* car.

geo- A prefix that is used at the beginning of words that refer to the whole of the world or to the Earth's surface. For example, *geology* is the study of the Earth's structure, surface, and origins.

gerund Another name for the *-ing* form when it is used as a noun.

grammar The rules of a language relating to the ways you can combine words to form sentences.

great- A prefix that is used before some nouns that refer to relatives. Nouns formed in this way refer to a relative who is a further generation away from you. For example, your *great-aunt* is the aunt of one of your parents.

H

hyper- A prefix that forms adjectives which refer to people or things which have a large amount of, or too much of a particular quality. For example, someone who is *hyperactive* has a large amount of energy and is very active.

hyphen A hyphen joins two or more words together, while a dash keeps them apart.

The rules governing the use of hyphens, are about the most contradictory and volatile in grammar. And yet their purpose is simple: to help us construct words to clarify meaning and avoid ambiguity. Take these two similar newspaper headlines:

MAN EATING TIGER SEEN NEAR MOTORWAY.
MAN-EATING TIGER SEEN NEAR MOTORWAY.

The first headline suggests that a hungry gourmet has decided to barbecue some choice jungle beast near a motorway, while the second could prove fatal should you be carelessly wandering along the hard shoulder. A hyphen has made all the difference.

Hyphens enable us to create useful compounds by uniting two or more associated words. Sometimes the marriage is permanent. A *book seller* became a *book-seller* and is now a *bookseller*.

Many hyphenated couplings exist primarily to obviate confusion. Have you ever seen a stick walking? Or shuddered at an ear splitting, or witnessed a room changing? Obviously not, but just in case of a misunderstanding we hyphenate: *walking-stick, ear-splitting, changing-room.*

Then there are hyphenated couples never destined to become permanent partners because of 'letter collision', which is visually disconcerting: *shell-like* (not shelllike); *semi-illiterate* (not semiilliterate); *de-ice* (not deice); *co-wrote* (not cowrote) – although we accept such unhyphenated words as *cooperative* and *coordination*.

Generally, hyphens are used after the prefixes *ex-* (*ex-cop*); *non-* (*non-starter*) and *self-* (*self-employed*). They are not usually required after *anti-* (*antifreeze*); *counter-* (*counterweight*); *co-* (*coreligionist*); *neo-* (*neoclassicism*); *pre-* (*prehensile*); and *un-* (*unconditional*). But there are some exceptions: *co-respondent* (to distinguish it from a somewhat misspelt correspondent!) and *re-creation* (not recreation).

hyperbole A deliberate overstatement: wild exaggeration used to make an emphatic point. For example, *he couldn't fight his way out of a paper bag*!

I

-ibility See -ability.

-ic A suffix that forms adjectives which indicate that something or someone is connected with a particular thing. For example, *photographic equipment* is equipment connected with photography.

-ication See -ation.

-icity A suffix that replaces *-ic* at the end of adjectives to form nouns referring to the state, quality, or behaviour described by the adjective. For example, *authenticity* refers to the quality of being authentic.

idiom A group of words whose meaning together is different from all the words taken individually. For example, *it's raining cats and dogs.*

if- clause See conditional clause.

-ify A suffix that is used at the end of verbs that refer to making something or someone different in some way. For example, if you *simplify* something, you make it easier to understand or you remove the things which make it complex.

il-, im-, in-, and **ir-** Prefixes that can be added to some words to form words which have the opposite meaning. For example, if an activity is *illegal*, it is not legal. If someone is *impatient*, they are not patient.

imagery The descriptive and figurative language used in a poem or a book.

imperative The form of a verb used when giving orders and commands, which is the same as its base form:
Come here!
Take two tablets every four hours.
Enjoy yourself.

impersonal Where it is used as an impersonal subject to introduce new information:
It's raining
It's ten o'clock.

indefinite article The determiners *a* and *an*.

indefinite pronoun A small group of pronouns including *someone* and *anything* which are used to refer to people or things without saying exactly who or what they are.

indirect object An object used with verbs that take two objects. For example, in *I gave him the pen* and *I gave the pen to him*, *him* is the indirect object and *pen* is the direct object.

indirect question A question used to ask for information or help:
Do you know where Anoop is?
I wonder which hotel it was.

indirect speech The words you use to report what someone has said, rather than using their actual words. Also called reported speech.

infinitive The base form of a verb:
I wanted to *go*.
She helped me *dig* the garden.

-ing A suffix that is added to verbs to make the *-ing* form, or present participle. Present participle forms are often used as adjectives describing a person or thing who is doing something. For example, a *sleeping baby* is a baby that is sleeping and an *amusing joke* is a joke that *amuses* people. Present participle forms are also used as nouns which refer to activities. For example, if you say you like *dancing*, you mean that you like to *dance*.

inter- A prefix that forms adjectives which refer to things that move, exist, or happen between two or more people or things. For example, *inter-city* trains travel between cities.

interjection A word that expresses a strong emotion, such as anger, surprise, or excitement. Interjections often stand alone rather than as part

of a sentence.
Some interjections express greetings:
Hello.
Congratulations!

Some interjections express agreement or disagreement:
Indeed.
No.

Some interjections express pain, anger, or annoyance:
Ouch!
Blast!

Some interjections express approval, pleasure, or excitement:
Bravo!
Hooray!

Some interjections express surprise or relief:
Wow!
Phew!

Sometimes an interjection is more like a noise than a word:
Sh!
Psst!

A group of words can be used together as an interjection:
Happy birthday!
Hey presto!

When an interjection does occur within a sentence, it is usually separated by commas or dashes:
I turned the key and, bingo, the engine started.

interrogative pronoun One of the pronouns *who, whose, whom, what* and *which*, when they are used to ask questions.

intransitive verb A verb which does not take an object::
She arrived.
I was yawning.

inverted comma Inverted commas or quotation marks mark the beginning and end of a speaker's exact words or thoughts:
"I would like some more," said Matthew.

Inverted commas are not used when a speaker's words are reported indirectly rather than in their exact form:
Matthew said that he would like some more.

Inverted commas can also be used to indicate the title of a book, piece of music, etc:
The class had been reading "The Little Prince".

Inverted commas are also used to draw attention to the fact that a word or phrase is being used in an unusual way, or that a word itself is the subject of discussion:
Braille allows a blind person to "see" with the fingers.
What rhymes with "orange"?

irony A form of humour in which you say the opposite of what you really mean.

irregular verb A verb that has three forms or five forms, or whose forms do not follow the normal rules.

ir- See il-.

-ise A suffix used at the end of many verbs to describe processes by which things or people are brought into a new state. For example, to *standardise* things means to change them so that they all have the same features.

-ish A suffix that forms adjectives which indicate that someone or something has a quality to a small extent. For example, if you say that something is *largish*, you mean it is fairly large, and something that is *yellowish* is slightly yellow in colour.

-ism A suffix that forms nouns which refer to particular beliefs, or to behaviour based on these beliefs. For example, *professionalism* is behaviour that is professional and *racism* is the beliefs and behaviour of a racist.

-ist A suffix that replaces *-ism* at the end of nouns to form nouns and adjectives. The nouns can refer to the people who have particular beliefs. For example, a *fascist* is someone who supports fascism. The adjectives indicate that something is related to or is based on particular beliefs. The

-ist suffix also forms nouns which refer to people who do a particular kind of work. For example, a *geologist* is someone who works in the field of geology. Similarly, the *-ist* suffix also forms nouns which refer to people who play a particular musical instrument, often as their job. For example, a *violinist* is someone who plays the violin.

-ity A suffix that forms nouns which refer to a particular state or quality. For example, *solidity* is the state or quality of being solid.

J

jargon Consists of words that are used in special or technical ways by particular groups of people, often making the language difficult to understand.

L

-less A suffix that forms adjectives which indicate that someone or something does not have a particular thing. For example, someone who is *childless* does not have any children.

link verb A verb which takes a complement rather than an object: *be, become, seem, appear.*

-logical See -ological.

-logist See -ologist.

-logy See -ology.

-ly A suffix that forms adverbs which indicate how something is done. For example, if someone whistles *cheerfully*, they whistle in a cheerful way.

M

macro- A prefix that is added to words in order to form new words that are technical and that refer to things which are large or involve the whole of something. For example *macroeconomic* means relating to the major, general features of a country's economy, such as the level of inflation or unemployment.

main clause A clause which does not depend on another clause, and is not part of another clause.

main verb All verbs which are not auxiliaries or modals.

mal- A suffix that forms words which refer to things that are bad or unpleasant, or that are unsuccessful or imperfect. For example, if a machine *malfunctions*, it does not work properly.

masculine Masculine nouns refer to male people and animals:
The *boy* put on his coat.

Common nouns may be either masculine or feminine. Other words in the sentence may tell us if they are male or female:
The *doctor* parked *his* car.
The *doctor* parked *her* car.

mega- A prefix that forms words which refer to units which are a million times bigger. For example, a *megawatt* is a million watts.

-ment A suffix forms nouns which refer to the process of making or doing something, or to the result of this process. For example, *assessment* is the process of assessing something or the judgment made as a result of assessing it.

metaphor An imaginative way of describing something as another thing, and so suggesting that it has the typical qualities of that other thing. For example, if you wanted to say that someone is shy, you might say that they are a *mouse*.

micro- A prefix that forms nouns which have *small* as part of their meaning. For example, a *micro-organism* is a very small living thing that you cannot see with the naked eye.

mid- A prefix that forms nouns and adjectives which refer to the middle part of a particular period of time, or the middle part of a particular place. For example, *mid-June* is the middle of June.

milli- A prefix that forms nouns which refer to units which are a thousand times smaller. For example, a *millimetre* is a thousandth of a metre.

mini- A prefix that forms nouns which refer to things which are a smaller version of something else. For example, a *minibus* is a small bus.

mis- A prefix that forms verbs and nouns which refer to something being done badly or wrongly. For example, if you *miscalculate* a figure, you wrongly calculate it.

modal A verb such as *can*, *might*, or *will*, which is always the first word in a verb group and is followed by the base form of a verb. Modals are used to express requests, offers, suggestions, wishes, intentions, politeness, possibility, probability, certainty, obligation etc.

mono- A prefix that forms nouns and adjectives which have *one* or *single* as part of their meaning. For example, *monogamy* is the custom of being married to only one person.

multi- A prefix that forms adjectives which refer to something that consists of many things of a particular kind. For example, a *multi-coloured* object has many different colours.

N

narco- A prefix that is added to words to form new words that relate to illegal narcotics. For example, a *narco-trafficker* is a person who illegally buys or sells narcotics.

-nd A suffix that is added to written numbers ending in 2, except for numbers ending in 12, in order to form ordinal numbers, for example *22nd February, 2nd edition*.

-ness A suffix that forms nouns which refer to a particular state or quality. For example, *gentleness* is the state or quality of being gentle.

negative A negative clause, question, sentence, or statement is one which has a negative word such as *not*, and indicates the absence or opposite of something, or is used to say that something is not the case:
I *don't* know you.
I'll *never* forget.

negative word A word such as *never, no, not, nothing,* or *nowhere,* which makes a clause, question, sentence, or statement negative.

neo- A prefix that forms nouns and adjectives which refer to modern versions or styles and particular groups of the past. For example, *neo-classical* architecture is based on ancient Greek or Roman architecture.

neuro- A prefix that is used to form words that refer to or relate to a nerve or the nervous system. For example, *neurology* is the study of the structure, function, and diseases of the nervous system.

neuter Neuter nouns refer to inanimate objects and abstract ideas:
The *kettle* will switch itself off.

non- A prefix that forms nouns and adjectives which refer to people or things that do not have a particular quality or characteristic. For example, a *non-smoker* does not smoke and a *non-fatal* accident is not fatal. It also forms nouns which refer to situations where a particular action has not taken place. For example, someone's *non-attendance* at a meeting is the fact of their not having attended the meeting.

non-defining relative clause A relative clause which gives more information about someone or something, but which is not needed to identify them because we already know who or what they are:
That's Mary, *who was at university with me.*

not A word that can turn most sentences into negatives if you want to express the opposite meaning:
Robbie was *not* feeling tired.

If a sentence already contains an auxiliary verb, such as *have, will, be,* or *must,* the word *not* should go after this verb:
She *has not* gone to the shops.

If the sentence does not already contain an auxiliary verb, a form of the verb *do* is added, and the word *not* is placed after this:
We *do not* expect to win.

In spoken and informal English, the ending *-n't* may be added to an auxiliary verb in place of *not*:
She *hasn't* gone to the shops.

noun A noun is a word that labels a person, a thing or an idea. In any sentence, the nouns will tell you which people or things are involved. They are sometimes called "naming words".

Common nouns are words which indicate every example of a certain type of thing. They begin with lower-case letters:
girl
city
picture

Proper nouns are words which give the name of a particular person, place, or object. They begin with capital letters:
Anna Jamieson
Los Angeles
The Mona Lisa

Some common nouns are **concrete nouns**. These are words that indicate things that you can touch:
cat
pen
apple

Other common nouns are **abstract nouns**. These are words that indicate things that you cannot touch:
beauty
ambition
popularity

Some common nouns are **collective nouns**. These are words that indicate a group or collection of things:
pack
bunch
flock

noun group   A group of words which acts as the subject, complement, or object of a verb, or as the object of a preposition.

number   Numbers tell you how many of a thing there are.

Cardinal numbers tell you the total number of a thing:
Three figures huddled in the doorway.

Ordinal numbers tell you the order of something. They often end with the letters *-th*:
Her *sixth* novel was the most successful yet.

O

object A noun group which refers to a person or thing that is affected by the action described by a verb. Compare with subject. Prepositions also have noun groups as objects.

object pronoun One of a set of pronouns including *me*, *him*, and *them*, which are used as the object of a verb or preposition. Object pronouns are also used as complements after *be*:
I hit *him*.
It's *me*.

-ological or **-logical** Suffixes which are used to replace *-ology* or *-logy* at the end of nouns in order to form adjectives that describe something as relating to a particular science or subject. For example, *biological* means relating to biology.

-ologist or **-logist** Suffixes which are used to replace *-ology* or *-logy* at the end of nouns in order to form other nouns that refer to people who are concerned with a particular science or subject. For example, a *biologist* is concerned with biology.

-ology or **-logy** Suffixes that are used at the end of some nouns that refer to a particular science or subject, for example *biology* or *sociology*.

onomatopoeia The use of words which sound like the thing that they represent. For example, *hiss* and *buzz*.

-or See *-er*.

ordinal number A number used to indicate where something comes in an order or sequence: *first, fifth, tenth, hundredth.*

-ous A suffix that forms adjectives which indicate that someone or something has a particular quality. For example, someone who is *courageous* shows courage.

out- A prefix that forms verbs which refer to an action as being done better by one person than by another. For example, if you can *outswim* someone, you can swim further or faster than they can.

over- A prefix that forms words which refer to a quality of action that exists or is done to great an extent. For example, if someone is being *over-cautious*, they are being too cautious.

P

pan- A prefix that is added to the beginning of adjectives and nouns to form other adjectives and nouns that describe something as being connected with all places or people of a particular kind. For example, a *pandemic* is an occurrence of a disease that affects many people over a very wide area.

para- A prefix that forms nouns and adjectives which refer to people or things which are similar to other things. For example, a *paramilitary* organisation is organized like an army, and a *paramedic* is a person whose training is similar to that of a nurse and who helps to do medical work. It also forms nouns and adjectives which refer to situations which are beyond or more important than normal. For example, a *paranormal* event cannot be explained by scientific laws and is thought to involve strange, unknown forces.

paragraph A section of writing. A paragraph starts on a new line.

parenthesis Material that has been added to the text, but could be omitted and still leave a meaningful sentence can be put in parenthesis, which can be marked off with commas, dashes and brackets. The uses of parenthises are:

Giving references
Buddhism is discussed in Chapter 7 (see pages 152-197).

Giving translations
The boat was called "La Ardilla Roja" (The Red Squirrel).

Adding information
One of the earliest dictionaries is that of Elisha Coles (London, 1685).

Offering explanation
Unable to follow the instructions in French and after nothing but trouble she returned the car (a Renault saloon) to the garage.

Afterthought
Travel by car, choose the cross-channel route that offers best value for money, and look out for bargains (like newspaper tokens. Last summer we scored a free hotel in France).

Clarification
The directive stated quite clearly (page 394, second paragraph) that the department would be closed from March 1.

Comment
Cruelty to animals (I noted a scene in which a donkey's tail was tied to a post, and another where a tin can with a lit firecracker in it was attached to a dog's tail) was a fairly common sight in children's comic papers in the 1920s.

Illustration
The candidate spent far too long discussing irrelevancies (20 minutes on the price of footwear; another ten on tax havens) with the inevitable result that most of us walked out.

To express an aside
She claims to be 35 (and pigs can fly).

To indicate options
Your document(s) will be returned in due course.

There is an important grammatical difference between parenthesising material within commas and within brackets. Generally, material enclosed by commas is still very much part of the sentence and should observe the grammatical conventions of that sentence. Bracketed material, on the other hand, is rather more distanced from the sentence into which it is inserted, and can assume its own punctuation.

part- A prefix that forms words which refer to something that is partly but not completely a particular thing. For example, *part-baked* bread is only partly baked.

part of speech Every word in the dictionary can be classified into a group. These groups are known as parts of speech. If we know which group a word belongs to, we can understand what sort of idea the word represents, and how it can be combined with other words to produce meaningful statements.

You can check the part of speech of any word by looking it up in the dictionary. The part of speech is given after the main entry word. The most common parts of speech in this guide are noun, verb, adjective, adverb, pronoun, preposition, interjection and conjunction.

participle A verb form used for making different tenses. Verbs have two participles, a present participle and a past participle.

particle An adverb or preposition which combines with verbs to form phrasal verbs.

passive voice The passive voice and the active voice are two different ways of presenting information in a sentence. The passive always uses a form of the auxiliary verb *to be* with the past participle of the verb. When a sentence is in the passive voice, the subject of the verb is affected by the action, rather than doing it:
The cat is being fed by Anna.
The mouse was chased by a cat.

It usually sounds more natural to use the active rather than the passive. However, it is sometimes better to use the passive if you want to avoid giving blame or if the name of the subject is not known:
The book has been mislaid.
We are being followed.

past form The form of a verb, often ending in -*ed*, which is used for the past simple tense.

past participle A verb form which is used to form perfect tenses and passives. Some past participles are also used as adjectives: *watched, broken, swum.*

past tense You can talk about events that have already happened by using simple past tenses or compound tenses.
The simple past tense is formed without any auxiliary verbs. It is usually formed by taking the dictionary form of the verb and adding the ending -*ed*. (If the verb already ends in -*e*, then you only need to add -*d*.)
I cook*ed* the dinner.
She lik*ed* fish.

You can also use compound tenses to talk about actions that have happened. One compound past tense is formed by using *was* or *were* in front of the main verb, and adding the ending -*ing*. This shows that an action happening in the past was continuous:
I was cook*ing* the dinner.
We were din*ing*.

Notice that if the verb ends in -*e*, the -*e* is dropped.

Another compound past tense is formed by using a form of the verb to *have* in front of the main verb, and adding the ending -*ed*. This shows that an action has been completed:
I have cook*ed* the dinner.
We have din*ed*.
Notice that if the verb already ends in -*e* you don't need to add one.

Another compound past tense is formed by using *had* in front of the main verb, and adding the ending -*ed*. This form shows that an action in the past had been completed before something else took place:
I had cook*ed* the dinner.
We had din*ed*.

Another compound past tense is formed by using *did* in front of the basic form of the verb. This can add emphasis:
We *did* enjoy that!

perfect tense see tense.

person One of the three classes of people who can be involved in something that is said. The person or people who are speaking or writing are called the first person (*I, we*). The person or people who are listening or reading are called the second person (*you*). The person, people or things that are being talked about are called the third person (*he, she, it, they*).

personal pronoun One of the group of words including *I, you*, and *me*, which are used to refer back to yourself, the people you are talking to, or the people or things you are talking about.

-phile A suffix that occurs at the end of words which refer to someone who has a very strong liking for people or things of a particular kind. For example, if you describe a non-British person as *Anglophile*, you mean that they admire Britain and British culture.

-phobe A suffix that occurs at the end of words which refer to someone who has a very strong irrational fear or hatred of people or things of a particular kind. For example, if you refer to someone as a *technophobe*, you mean that they do not like new technology, such as computers or mobile telephones, and are afraid to use it.

-phobia A suffix that occurs at the end of words which refer to a very strong irrational fear or hatred of something. For example, someone who suffers from *claustrophobia* feels very uncomfortable or anxious when they are in small or enclosed places.

-phobic A suffix that occurs at the end of words which describe something relating to a strong, irrational fear or hatred of people or things of a particular kind. For example, you describe a place or situation as *claustrophobic* when it makes you feel uncomfortable and unhappy because you are enclosed or restricted.

phrase A phrase is a group of words which combine together but is not usually capable of standing on its own to describe an idea or situation. It requires additional words to form a meaningful sentence:
She drank *a cup of tea*.
I was reading a book.

Some phrases act as nouns:
A stack of newspapers lay on the floor.
My sister's friend lives in Canada.

Some phrases act as verbs. Verb phrases often contain an auxiliary verb. They may also contain adverbs:
She *was always complaining* about the buses.
He *used to play* the piano.

Some phrases act as adjectives. When words combine to act as an adjective, they are usually hyphenated if they occur before the noun:
The food here is *of the highest quality*.
He asked for an *up-to-the-minute* report.

Some phrases act as adverbs. Adverb phrases often begin with a preposition:
She disappeared *in the blink of an eye*.
They played *with great gusto*.

Some phrases are acceptable as substitutes for sentences. Although they do not contain a subject and a verb, they can be understood on their own:
Happy Birthday!
Good morning.
All right?

phrasal verb A combination of a verb and a particle, which together have a different meaning to the verb on its own: *back down, hand over, look forward to.*

plural Most nouns can exist in either the singular or plural. The singular form of the noun is used to mean only one instance of a thing. This is the main form given in the dictionary:
one book
a raven

The plural form of the noun is used to mean more than one instance of a thing. The plural form is given in the dictionary in smaller type after the main form:
two books
some ravens

The plural form of the noun is usually formed by adding the letter *-s* to the singular:
book → *books*
raven → *ravens*

Words that end in *-s, -z, -x, -ch,* or *-sh* in the singular are made plural by adding the letters *-es*:
cross → *crosses*
box → *boxes*

Words that end in a consonant + *-y* in the singular are made plural by removing the *-y* and adding *-ies*:
pony → *ponies*
party → *parties*

Words that end in *-ife* in the singular are made plural by removing the *-fe* and adding *-ves*:
knife → *knives*
life → *lives*

Some words that end in *-f* in the singular are made plural by removing the *-f* and adding *-ves*. Other words that end in *-f* in the singular are made plural by simply adding *-s*:
hoof → *hooves*
roof → *roofs*
Be careful not to use an apostrophe (') when you add an *-s* to make a plural.

Irregular Plurals

Some words that have come to English from a foreign language have plurals that do not end in -s.

Some words that came into English from French have plurals ending in -x:
bureau → *bureaux*
gateau → *gateaux*

Some words that came into English from Italian have plurals ending in -i:
paparazzo → *paparazzi*
graffito → *graffiti*

Some words that came into English from Hebrew have plurals ending in -im:
cherub → *cherubim*
kibbutz → *kibbutzim*

Some words that came into English from Latin have plurals ending in -i, -a, or -ae:
cactus → *cacti*
medium → *media*
formula → *formulae*

Some words that came into English from Ancient Greek have plurals ending in -a:
phenomenon → *phenomena*
criterion → *criteria*

The plural forms of a few words are not formed according to any regular rule. However, there are very few words like this. Here are some of the most common ones: *child, children; deer, deer; fish, fish* or *fishes; foot, feet; man, men; mouse, mice; ox, oxen; sheep, sheep; woman, women.*

plural noun A noun which is normally used only in the plural form: *trousers, scissors.*

poly- A prefix that forms nouns and adjectives which have *many* as part of their meaning. For example, a *polysyllabic* word contains many syllables.

positive A positive clause, question, sentence, or statement is one which does not contain a negative word such as *not.*

possessive case   The possessive case is formed by adding an apostrophe and the letter -*s* to the dictionary form of the word.

The possessive is used when a noun indicates a person or thing that owns another person or thing:
The *cat's fur* was wet.
The *doctor's cat* was called Joey.

If the noun is plural and already ends in -*s*, the possessive is formed by simply adding an apostrophe:
The vet often trims *cats' claws*.
Doctors' surgeries make me nervous.

The possessive can also be shown by using the word *of* in front of the noun. This is usually used when you are talking about something that is not alive or cannot be touched:
We climbed to the top *of the hill*.
He is a master *of disguise*.

When a possessive is not followed by another noun, it refers to the place where that person lives or works:
I am going to stay at my *aunt's*.
I bought a loaf at the *baker's*.

possessive determiner   One of the determiners *my, your, his, her, its, our*, or *their*, which is used to show that one person or thing belongs to another: *your car*.

possessive pronoun   One of the pronouns *mine, yours, hers, his, ours*, or *theirs*.

post-   A prefix that forms words that refer to something that takes place after a particular date, period, or event. For example, a *post-Christmas* sale takes place just after Christmas.

pre-   A prefix that forms words that refer to something that takes place before a particular date, period, or event. For example, a *pre-election* rally takes place just before an election.

prefix   Prefixes are beginnings of words, which have a regular and predictable meaning.

preposition A word such as *by, with* or *from*, which is always followed by a noun group.

preposition Usually acts as a joining word, like a conjunction, but it also always adds extra information to the words or sentence element it links:
We went *to* the beach.
He rose *at* dawn.
She shopped *for* some shoes.

From these examples you will notice that the prepositions have a particular ability to unite two elements in terms of space (*to*), time (*at*), and reason (*for*):

Space	*above, between, over, into, near, beside, along, amid*
Time	*after, at, before, during, since, until, past*
Others	*as,* for, *in, to, but, by, with, without*
Complex	*instead of, other than, in front of, up to, owing to*

Prepositions can create phrases that function adverbially or adjectivally:

Adverial phrase   The farmer *drove through the gate*
She was *sitting in the alcove*
Eric vanished *with the cash*

Adjectival phrase He drove along the road *to the farm*
She sat on the seat *in the alcove*
Eric was one *of the crooks*

In the first three sentences the adverbial phrases are telling us *where* the farmer drove, *where* she sat, and *how* Eric vanished. In each of the other sentences the phrases modify the nouns *road* and *seat* and the pronoun *one*.

Here is a sentence containing three prepositions, all functioning as adverbs:

adjective	**prep. phrase**	**noun**	**verb**	**preposition**	**prep. phrase**
According	*to the movie*	*the hero*	*fell*	*from the cliffs*	*into the sea.*

Another interesting thing about prepositions is that when you use one in a sentence, it can be replaced only by another preposition:
She found a mouse *in* the house.
She found a mouse *under* the house.
She found a mouse *near* the house.

You could substitute any number of prepositions – *beside, inside, behind, beneath* – but only with some difficulty could you substitute any other class of words.

present participle See -*ing* form.

present tense You can talk about events that are happening now by using simple tenses or compound tenses.

The simple present tense is formed by using the verb on its own, without any auxiliary verbs. For the first and second person, and for all plural forms, the simple present tense of the verb is the same as the main form given in the dictionary:
I cook the dinner.

For the third person singular, however, you need to add an -*s* to the dictionary form to make the simple present tense:
He cooks the dinner.

You can also talk about an event that is happening in the present by using compound tenses. Compound tenses are formed by adding an auxiliary verb to a form of the main verb. The most common compound present tense is formed by putting a form of the verb to be in front of the main verb, and adding the ending -*ing*. This shows that the action is going on at the present time and is continuous:
I am listening to the radio.

You can also talk about the present using a form of the verb *to do* in front of the basic form of the verb. This can add emphasis:
I do like fish.

pro- A prefix that forms adjectives which refer to people who strongly support a particular person or thing. For example, if you are *pro-democracy*, you support democracy.

progressive tense Another name for continuous tense.

pronoun A pronoun is a word that is used in place of a noun. Pronouns may be used instead of naming a person or thing.

Personal pronouns replace the subject or object of a sentence:
She caught a fish.
The nurse reassured *him*.

Reflexive pronouns replace the object when it is the same person or thing as the subject:
Matthew *saw himself* in the mirror.

Demonstrative pronouns replace the subject or object when you want to show where something is:
That is a nice jacket.
Have you seen *this*?

Possessive pronouns replace the subject or object when you want to show who owns it:
The blue car is *mine*.
Hers is a strange story.

Relative pronouns replace a noun to link two different parts of the sentence:
Do you know the man *who* lives next door?
I watched a programme *that* I had recorded yesterday.

Interrogative pronouns ask questions:
What are you doing?

Indefinite pronouns replace a subject or object to talk about a broad or vague range of people or things:
Everybody knew the exercise was a waste of time.
Some say he cheats at cards.

proper noun A noun which is the name of a particular person, place, organization, or building. Proper nouns are always written with a capital letter: *Mehmet, Edinburgh, the United Nations, Christmas.*

proto- A prefix that is used to form adjectives and nouns which indicate that something is in the early stages of its development. For example, a *prototype* is a new type of machine or device which is not yet ready to be made in large numbers and sold.

pseudo- A prefix that forms nouns and adjectives which refer to something which is not really what is seems or claims to be. For example, a *pseudo-science* is something that claims to be a science, but is not.

psycho- A prefix that is added to words in order to form other words which describe or refer to things connected with the mind or with mental processes. For example, a *psychoanalyst* is someone who treats people who have mental problems.

Q

qualifier A word or group of words, such as an adjective, prepositional phrase, or relative clause, which comes after a noun and gives more information about it:
the person involved.
a book with a blue cover.
the shop that I went into.

question Questions are used to ask for information.
A question has a question mark at the end of the sentence:
What is your name?

Questions are often introduced by a questioning word such as *what, who, where, when, why,* or *how*:
Where do you live?

If a sentence does not already contain an auxiliary verb, a form of the auxiliary verb *do* may be placed at the start to turn it into a question:
Does Sima have a sister?

If there is already an auxiliary verb in the sentence, you can turn it into a question by reversing the word order so the auxiliary verb comes before the subject instead of after it:
Are you going to the swimming baths?
Must they keep doing that?

A question can also be made by adding a phrase, such as *isn't it* or *don't you*, on to the end of a statement:
It is hot today, isn't it?
You like chocolate, don't you?

question mark A question mark is used to warn the reader that the preceding word or statement is interrogative, or of doubtful validity. A sentence that asks a question directly requires a question mark, but a sentence that poses an indirect question does not:

Direct question *Are you going to the match?*

Indirect question *I asked him if he was going to the match.*

This looks fairly simple but sometimes an indirect question can be disguised:

Why should allegations that go unchallenged in America be the subject of legal action in Britain, asks Roy Greenslade.
Not a question mark in sight. Now look at this similar example:
I wonder how many people will be homeless this Christmas?

The first example seems to be shouting for a question mark after Britain, but if you study the sentence carefully you will see that it is just a novel form of an indirect question. We could rewrite it more clearly as an indirect question:

Roy Greenslade asks why should allegations that go unchallenged in America be the subject of legal action in Britain.
Or, in the form of a reported direct question:
Roy Greenslade asks, 'Why should allegations that go unchallenged in America be the subject of legal action in Britain?'

The second example is also an indirect question, so why is it followed by a question mark? This is because many writers fall into this error; the sentence should end with a full stop. Either that, or rewrite the sentence to include a direct question:
I wondered, 'How many people will be homeless this Christmas?'

Generally question marks come at the end of sentences but sometimes can be inserted within them:

Perhaps – who knows? – there may in the future be some belated recognition for his services to mankind.

Don't forget that, no matter how long your sentence is, if there is a direct question contained in it, the question mark is still required:

Is it not curious that 'Lourdes', which within a year of publication sold over 200,000 copies, had critical acclaim poured over it like champagne and which provoked such a furore that it was instantly placed on the Vatican's Index of prohibited books, is not still widely read today?

question tag An auxiliary or modal with a pronoun, which is used to turn a statement into a question:
He's very friendly, isn't he?
I can come, can't I?

quotation There are two ways of writing what people say. You can write down the exact words that are spoken. This is called direct speech. The second way is to write down the meaning of what they say without using the exact words. This is called indirect speech or reported speech.

When you use direct speech, the exact words spoken go into quotation marks:
Robbie said, "Thank you very much for the prize."

The sentence will contain a main verb which indicates speaking, such as *say, tell, ask,* or *answer.* The words contained in quotation marks begin with a capital letter. If there is no other punctuation, they are separated from the rest of the sentence by a comma:

"This is the best picture," said the judge.

When you use indirect or reported speech, there is a subordinate clause which reports the meaning of what was said.

The judge said that Robbie's picture was the best.

When the reported words are a statement, the clause that reports them is usually introduced by that. The main clause usually contains a verb such as *say, tell, explain,* or *reply*:

The judge said that Robbie should win first prize.

Sometimes the word that can be left out:
The judge said Robbie should win first prize.

quotation marks The most common problem people have is whether to use single ('*single*') marks or double ("*double*") marks:
Heather said flatly, '*I never want to see him again.*'
Heather said flatly, "*I never want to see him again.*"

Whether you use double or single marks you need to be aware of the convention for enclosing a quoted passage within another. If you are a single-quote writer, an additional direct speech quote within your first quote must be enclosed within double marks (or vice versa):

The sales assistant said, 'We have them only in grey and blue but yesterday my boss told me, "I don't know why they don't make them in other colours".'

On the rare occasions where it is found necessary to have a third quote within a second quote in the same sentence, the formula is *single/double/single*, or *double/single/double*.

Quoting direct speech

When we read a newspaper report or story we want to know when we're reading reported or paraphrased speech and when we're reading words actually spoken. Quotation marks allow us to differentiate between the two forms:

Mr Murphy said that in his view the value of the pound would drop towards the end of the year. '*I also believe most European currencies will follow suit*,' he added.

This tells us that the writer has summarised the first part of the statement in his own words, and we have to accept that his summary is a correct interpretation of what Mr Murphy said. But we should have no doubts about the accuracy of the second part of the statement because the quote marks have signalled that the words are those actually spoken by Mr Murphy.

When you are quoting direct speech you must ensure that the words enclosed by your quotation marks are exactly those spoken. Not approximately, but exactly. It is also vital to make sure your reader knows who is responsible for the quoted statement. This is usually accomplished by what is called a reporting clause, which can introduce the statement or follow it or even interrupt it:

Jones stated, 'I am innocent and I can easily prove it.'
'I am innocent and I can easily prove it,' *Jones stated*.
'I am innocent,' *Jones stated*, 'and I can easily prove it.'

Another point to remember is that when quoted speech is interrupted by a reporting clause, two rules apply. If the quoted statement is interrupted at the end of a sentence it should be finished with a comma and resumed with a capital letter:
'*I knew I'd seen that bird before*,' said Gavin. '*It was a cormorant, wasn't it?*'

But if the speech is interrupted mid-sentence, it should be resumed in lower case:
'*Don't you agree*,' asked Gavin, '*that the bird over there is a cormorant?*'

How to close quotations

It is easy to remind writers not to forget to close their quotation; like enclosing brackets, the marks always operate in pairs. Look at this example:

Louis then asked her, 'Do you think I'm ill'?

Do you place the question mark outside the quotation mark that closes the direct speech, or inside?

Louis then asked her, 'Do you think I'm ill?'

The answer is that it depends on the relationship between the quotation and the sentence that contains it. The rule is well worth remembering: Punctuation marks (full stops, commas, question and exclamation marks, etc.) go inside the final quotation make if they relate to the quoted words, but outside, if they relate to the whole sentence.

In our example, the question mark relates only to the quoted statement, *'Do you think I'm ill?'* and so it rightly belongs inside the final quote mark, not outside.

But let's change the sentence slightly:

Should Louis have asked her, *'Do you think I'm ill'?*

Here, if you remember the rule, you can see that the question is an essential part of the whole sentence, and so the question mark outside the final quote mark is correct. To be pedantic, the sentence should properly be written like this:

Should Louis have asked her, *'Do you think I'm ill?'?*

Here you see that the quotation has its own question mark inside the final quote mark (quite correctly), and the overall sentence has its mark outside (again correctly). But the two piggybacked question marks look a bit silly and everyone accepts that in a case like this the inside question mark can be dropped without causing confusion.

With full stops, however, a different principle applies. If the quotation is a complete sentence that would normally end with a full stop, the stop outside the final quote marks is omitted and the whole sentence ended with a stop inside the final quote mark:

Wrong *Louis tried to tell her, 'I think I'm ill.'.*

Incorrect *Louis tried to tell her, 'I think I'm ill.'*

R

-rd A suffix that is added to written numbers ending in 3, except for numbers ending in 13, in order to form ordinal numbers, for example, *September 3rd, the 23rd London Marathon.*

re- A prefix that forms verbs and nouns which refer to an action or process being repeated. For example, if you *re*-read something, you read it again.

reciprocal verb A verb which describes an action which involves two people doing the same thing to each other:
I met you at the dance.
We've met one another before.
They met in the street.

reflexive pronoun A pronoun ending in *-self* or *-selves*, such as *myself* or *themselves*, which you use as the object of a verb when you want to say that the object is the same person or thing as the subject of the verb in the same clause: *He hurt himself.*

reflexive verb A verb which is normally used with a reflexive pronoun as object:
He contented himself with the thought that he had the only set of keys.

regular verb A verb that has four forms, and follows the normal rules.

relative clause A subordinate clause which gives more information about someone or something mentioned in the main clause.

relative pronoun Relative pronouns are used to replace a noun which links two different parts of a sentence. The relative pronouns are *who*, *whom*, *whose*, *which*, and *that*.

Relative pronouns always refer back to a word in the earlier part of the sentence. The word they refer to is called the antecedent:
I have a friend who lives in Rome.
We could go to a place that I know.

The forms *who*, *whom*, and *whose* are used when the antecedent is a person. *Who* indicates the subject of the verb, while *whom* indicates the object of the verb:
It was *the same person who* saw me yesterday.
It was *the person whom* I saw yesterday.

The distinction between *who* and *whom* is often ignored in everyday English, and *who* is often used as the object:
It was *the person who* I saw yesterday.

Whom is used immediately after a preposition. However, if the preposition is separated from the relative pronoun, who is usually used:
He is *a man in whom* I have great confidence.
He is *a man who* I have great confidence in.

Whose is the possessive form of the relative pronoun. It can refer to things as well as people:
Anna has *a sister whose* name is Rosie.
I found *a book whose* pages were torn.

Which is only used when the antecedent is not a person:
We took *the road which* leads to the sea.

That refers to things or people. It is never used immediately after a preposition, but it can be used if the preposition is separated from the relative pronoun:
It was *a film that* I had little interest *in*.

reported question A question which is reported using a report structure rather than the exact words used by the speaker.

reported speech The words you use to report what someone has said, rather than using their actual words. Also called indirect speech.

reporting verb A verb which describes what people say or think: *suggest, say, wonder*.

rhetoric Speech or writing that is intended to impress people.

rhyme Words with a similar sound are said to rhyme. For example, *Sally rhymes with valley*.

rhythm A regular movement or beat.

S

second person See person.

semi-modal A term used by some grammars to refer to the verbs *dare*, *need*, and *used to*, which behave like modals in some structures.

semi- A prefix that forms nouns and adjectives which refer to people and things that are partly, but not completely, in a particular state. For example, if you are *semi-conscious*, you are partly, but not wholly, conscious.

semicolon A semicolon has a number of practical grammatical and stylistic functions:

To join words, word groups and sentences

Occasionally we find ourselves writing a long sentence with too many connecting words such as *and*, *but* and *also*, with the danger of getting into an impossible tangle:

The history of the semicolon and colon is one of confusion because there are no precise rules governing their use and, furthermore, many writers would argue that both marks are really stylistic rather than parenthetical devices, and can in any case be easily replaced by commas, stops and dashes, and there the argument rests.

There's nothing grammatically wrong with that, but it is unwieldy and unappealing to both eye and mind. Many writers would, without hesitation, recast it as two or more separate sentences:

The history of the semicolon and colon is one of confusion. There are no precise rules governing their use. Many writers argue that both marks are really stylistic rather than parenthetical devices which can easily be replaced by commas, stops and dashes. And there the argument rests.

The use of full stops to achieve shorter sentences can aid understanding, and that is certainly the case here. But some writers, feeling that the original long sentence is, after all, about a single subject and should therefore be kept as a whole and not split apart, would turn to the semicolon to achieve unity of thought without making things hard for the reader:

The history of the semicolon and colon is one of confusion; there are no precise rules governing their use; many writers argue that both marks are really stylistic rather than parenthetical devices and that they can easily be replaced by commas, stops and dashes; and there the argument rests.

To separate word groups already containing commas

Any sentence that is essentially a list should be crystal clear and easily read. Most 'sentence lists' adequately separate the items with commas, but sometimes the items themselves are groups containing commas and require semicolons for clarity. These two examples illustrate just how handy semicolons can be:

Those present included Mr and Mrs Allison, their daughters Sarah, Megan and Sue; the Smith twins; Reg and Paul Watson; Joyce, Helen and Bill Hobson; etc.

The line-up consisted of Bix Beiderbecke, cornet; Al Grande, trombone; George Johnson, tenor sax; Bob Gillette, banjo; Dick Voynow, piano, and Vic Moore on drums.

To restore order to sentences suffering from 'comma riot'

Here's a longish but reasonably accomplished sentence spoiled by 'comma riot':

His main aims in life, according to Wilma, were to achieve financial independence, to be powerfully attractive, not only to women but in particular to rich ladies, to eat and drink freely without putting on weight, to remain fit, vital and young-looking beyond his eightieth birthday and, last but not least, to not only read, but fully understand, Professor Stephen Hawking's 'A Brief History of Time'.

Many professional writers would defend this sentence, despite its eleven commas. But others, perhaps more concerned with clarity than rhythm, would suggest that some of the thoughts at least should be separated by the longer pauses provided by semicolons:

His main aims in life, according to Wilma, were to achieve financial independence; to be powerfully attractive, not only to women but in particular to rich ladies; to eat and drink freely without putting on weight; to remain fit, vital and young-looking beyond his eightieth birthday and, last but not least, to not only read but fully understand Professor Stephen Hawking's 'A Brief History of Time'.

To provide pauses before certain adverbs

There are certain adverbs and conjunctions that require a preceding pause, but one longer and stronger than that provided by a comma. Look at this example:

With a comma *It was a beautiful car, moreover it was economical to run.*

With a semicolon *It was a beautiful car; moreover it was economical to run.*

You can see and hear that need for a substantial pause before *moreover*, can't you?

A comma is wrong on both grammatical and rhetorical counts. Here's another example; read it and note your instinctive pause before *nevertheless*:

Joe claimed he'd beaten the bookies on every race; nevertheless he was broke as usual when he left the track.

Watch out for *therefore, however, besides, also, moreover, furthermore, hence, consequently* and *subsequently*; in many constructions they will require a preceding semicolon.

To induce a mild shock or make a joke

Semicolons can help the writer emphasise contrast and incongruity. For a woman to remark,

I thought his wife was lovely but that her dress was in poor taste.

would be rather too subtle. Here's what she might wish she'd said with the tart use of a mental semicolon:
I loved his wife; pity about the frock.

'semi'-question One very common use of the direct question is in the form of a polite request:

Would you let me know if either Monday or Tuesday next week will be suitable?

There is little doubt that the question mark is required; it is after all a straightforward question directed at someone. But here's a similar request-question:

Would you be good enough to ensure that in future cars and other vehicles belonging to non-staff are parked outside the gates.

Well, what is it – a request or a question? It is in fact both: part question, part demand, and writer and reader both sense that a question mark would weaken its authority. Look at these examples – all questions but all reasonably comfortable without a question mark:
You're not going to give in yet, I trust.
I hope you're not calling me a liar.
I wonder if I might borrow the car tomorrow.

In these cases, the expressions of personal feeling – *I trust, I hope* and *I wonder* – tend to undermine the question content of the statements. If you wrote *You're not going to give in yet?* or *May I borrow the car tomorrow?* you'd unhesitatingly finish with question marks. But there are some questions that look quite strange with a question mark:
How dare you? → *How dare you!*

Here the expression is more an angry exclamation than a query, and a question mark would, in most similar cases, seem inappropriate.

sentence The different types of word can go together to make sentences. A sentence is a group of words which expresses an idea or describes a situation.

Sentences begin with a capital letter:
The child was sleeping.

Sentences usually end with a full stop:
Deepa lives in Lisbon.

If a sentence is a question, it ends with a question mark instead of a full stop:
Where is my purse?

If a sentence is an exclamation of surprise, anger, or excitement, it ends with an exclamation mark instead of a full stop:
You must be joking!

Sentences have a subject, which indicates a person or thing. The rest of the sentence usually says something about the subject. The subject is usually the first word or group of words in a sentence:
Deepa laughed.
Robbie likes bananas.

Most sentences have a verb. The verb says what the subject of the sentence is doing or what is happening to the subject. The verb usually follows immediately after the subject:
Tarak *smiled*.

Simple Sentences, Compound Sentences, and Complex Sentences

Simple sentences consist of only one main clause, and no subordinate clause:
Anna fed the cat.

The subject of a simple sentence is the person or thing that the sentence is about. It usually comes at the start of the sentence. The subject may be a noun, a pronoun, or a noun phrase:
We often go to the cinema.

The remaining part of the sentence is called the predicate. The predicate says something about the subject:
Anna *likes to go swimming.*
She *is a strong swimmer.*
A ginger cat *was sitting on the stair.*

Compound sentences consist of two or more main clauses joined together by a conjunction. Both clauses are equally important:
Anna likes to go swimming, but Matthew likes to go fishing.

Complex sentences consist of a main clause with one or more subordinate clauses joined to it.

Numerous subordinate clauses can be added to a main clause:
After looking at all the pictures, the judges gave the first prize, *which was a silver trophy*, to Robbie, *because his work was the best.*

shall and will   The verbs *shall* and *will* have only one form. They do not have a present form ending in -*s*, and they do not have a present participle, a past tense, or a past participle.

These verbs are used as auxiliary verbs to form the future tense:
We shall arrive on Thursday.
She will give a talk about Chinese history.

People used to use *shall* to indicate the first person, and *will* to indicate the second person and the third person. However, this distinction is often ignored now:

I shall see you on Sunday.
I will see you on Sunday.

Shall is always used in questions involving I and we. *Will* is avoided in these cases:
Shall I put the cat out?
Shall we dance?

Will is always used when making polite requests, giving orders, and indicating persistence. *Shall* is avoided in these cases:
Will you please help me?
Will you be quiet!
She will keep going on about Al Pacino.

short form A form in which one or more letters are omitted and two words are joined together, for example an auxiliary or modal and *not*, or a subject pronoun and an auxiliary or modal: *aren't, couldn't, he'd, I'm, it's, she's.*

-sion and **-tion** See -ation.

similie An expression in which a person or thing is described as being similar to someone else. For example, *He's as white as a sheet.*

simple tense A present or past tense formed without using an auxiliary verb: I wait, she sang etc. See tense.

singular The form of a count noun or verb which is used to refer to or talk about one person or thing:
A dog was in the back of the car.
That woman is my mother.

singular noun A noun which is normally used only in the singular form: *the sun, a bath.*

speech marks See quotation marks.

spelling Here are a few tips on how to improve your spelling:
1) Learn the basic rules of spelling (*see* below).
2) Use mnemonics, which are jingles or patterns that jog your memory to help you to remember words that you find it difficult to spell. Examples are:
There's **a rat** in sep**arat**e
It is necessary to have one collar (**c**) and two socks (**ss**)
3) Break down the word into smaller parts and learn each small part separately.
4) Visualise a difficult word. Try to remember its letters and the shape they make. This will give you a feel for what looks right or wrong when you write it down.
5) Exaggerate the pronunciation of the word in your head. Sound out all the letters, including any silent letters.
6) Look at the word, cover it up, attempt to write it down, then check to see if you are correct. Keep doing this until you spell the word correctly.
7) Write out the word many times in your own handwriting until you feel it flows without you hesitating.
8) If you spell a word wrongly, make a note of the error. You can learn to recognise the mistakes you tend to make and so prevent yourself from repeating them.
9) Make a habit of looking up any word that you are not absolutely sure about in a dictionary.

Spelling rules
Here are some basic spelling rules. If you recognise and remember these rules, it will help you to spell a difficult or unfamiliar word.

1) a) A final silent *e* is dropped when an ending that begins with a vowel is added. For example:

abbreviate + ion → abbreviat + ion → abbreviation
argue + able → argu + able → arguable
fascinate + ing → fascinat + ing → fascinating

b) This *e* is retained for the endings *-ce* or *-ge* when these letters keep a soft second. For example:

change + able → changeable
courage + ous → courageous
outrage + ous → outrageous

2) When the adverb suffix -*ly* is added to an adjective that ends in a consonant followed by -*le*, the -*le* is usually dropped. For example:
gentle + *ly* → *gent* + *ly* → *gently*
idle + *ly* → *idl* + *ly* → *idly*
subtle + *ly* → *subtl* + *ly* → *subtly*

3) When an ending that begins with a vowel is added to a word that ends in a single vowel plus a consonant, the consonant is doubled if the stress is on the end of the word or if the word has only one part. For example:

admit + *ance* → *admitt* + *ance* → *admittance*
begin + *ing* → *beginn* + *ing* → *beginning*
equip + *ed* → *eqipp* + *ed* → *equipped*

4) When an ending that begins with a vowel is added to a word that ends in a single vowel plus -*l*, the -*l* is doubled. For example:

cancel + *ation* → *cancell* + *ation* → *cancellation*
excel + *ent* → *excell* + *ent* → *excellent*
fulfil + *ing* → *fulfill* + *ing* → *fulfilling*

5) When an ending that begins with *e*, *i*, or *y* is added to a word that ends in *c*, a *k* is also added to the *c* to keep its hard sound. For example:

panic + *ing* → *panick* + *ing* → *panicking*
An exception is *arc*, *arced*, *arcing*.

6) When the adjective suffix -*ous* or -*ary* is added to a word that ends in -*our*, the *u* of the -*our* is dropped. For example:

glamour + *ous* → *glamor* + *ous* → *glamorous*
honour + *ary* → *honor* + *ary* → *honorary*
humour + *ous* → *humor* + *ous* → *humorous*

7) When an ending is added to a word that ends in a consonant plus *y*, the *y* changes to *i* (unless the ending added already begins with *i*) For example:

beauty + *ful* → *beauti* + *ful* → *beautiful*
carry + *age* → *carri* + *age* → *carriage*
woolly + *er* → *woolli* + *er* → *woollier*

8) a) The plural of a word that ends in a consonant plus *y* is made by changing the *y* to *i* and adding -*es*, for example:

accessory → *accessori* + *es* → *accessories*
diary → *diari* +*es* → *diaries*

b) The plural of a word that ends in a vowel plus *y* is made by adding *s*. For example:

jersey + s → jerseys
journey + s → journeys

c) The plural of a word that ends in *-s, -x, -z, -sh* or *-ch* is made by adding *-es*. For example:

bus + es → buses
focus + es → foucuses

d) The plural of a word that ends in *-eau* is made by adding *s* or *x*. For example:

bureau + s → bureaus or
bureau + x → bureaux
gateau + s → gateaus or
gateau + x → gateaux

9) When *al-* is added as a prefix at the beginning of a word to make a new word, it is spelt with one *l*. For example:

al + ready → already
al + though → although
al + together → altogether

10) The suffix *-ful* is always spelt with one *l*. For example:

faithful, grateful, hopeful

11) The 'uss' sound at the end of an adjective is almost always spelt *-ous*. For example:

courageous, courteous, luscious

12) *i* before *e* except after *c*, when they make the sound 'ee'. For example:

fierce, niece, relieve but
ceiling, deceive, receive

13) a) The name or names of areas on the map begin with a capital letter:

Britain, Mediterranean

b) The name of a religious group or its teachings begins with a capital letter:

Buddhism

square bracket The square bracket has an entirely different function from that of parenthesis: words enclosed within them are not intended to be part of a sentence, but as an editorial or authorial interjection:

It was a matter of opinion that if offered the position, he [Professor Khan] would most likely refuse it on moral grounds.

This sentence came at the end of a very long paragraph; the professor's name had been mentioned at the beginning, but other names and much discussion followed so that the late reference to *he* was in danger of being misunderstood. The editor therefore inserted the name [*Professor Khan*] in square brackets as a reminder and also to indicate that the intervention was the editor's and not the author's.

One of the most common uses of square brackets is to enclose the adverb *sic* (from the Latin *sicut*, meaning *just as*) to indicate that incorrect or doubtful matter is quoted exactly from the original:

Pink and yellow concubines [sic] climbed in great profusion up the trellis.
Miss Patricia Wall Wall [sic] with her fiance Mr Gerald Kleeman.

The second example was a caption under a photograph of the newly engaged couple; The Times wanted to make sure that readers understood that '*Wall Wall*' really was the young lady's surname and not a misprint.

-st A suffix that is added to written numbers ending in *1* except for numbers ending in 11, in order to form ordinal numbers, for example, *1st August 1993*.

stroke Known as the virgule, slash and oblique, it has a few limited uses in texts:

To indicate options *It depends upon how he/she behaves. The situation calls for guile and/or force.*

To separate lines of verse *The mist as it rises / touched with gold of the morning / Veils over the sadness / and lifts, soaring …*

To abbreviate *A/c = account; C/o = care of; km/hr = kilometres per hour.*

With the advent of the Internet, however, along with the *at* symbol (@), it has gained importance as an integral part of Internet addresses. In this context it is called the *forward slash*, to differentiate it from the backslash, which is used in some computers' operating systems.

sub- A prefix that forms nouns which refer to things that are part of a larger thing. For example, a *subcommittee* is a small committee made up of members of a larger committee. It also forms adjectives which refer to people or things that are inferior. For example, *substandard* living conditions are inferior to normal living conditions.

subject The noun group in a clause that refers to the person or thing who does the action expressed by the verb: *We were going shopping.*

subject pronoun One of the set of pronouns including *I*, *she*, and *they*, which are used as the subject of a verb.

subjunctive A term used to describe the base form of a verb or *were* when used in a clause to express a wish or a suggestion:
He asked that they be removed.
I wish I were somewhere else.

subordinate clause A clause which must be used with a main clause and is not usually used alone, for example a time clause, conditional clause, relative clause, or result clause, and which begins with a subordinating conjunction such as *because or while*.

suffixes A word ending which can be added to words, usually to make a new word with a similar meaning but different part of speech.

super- A prefix that forms nouns and adjectives which refer to people and things that are larger, better, or more advanced than others. For example, a *super-fit* athlete is extremely fit, and a *supertanker* is a very large tanker.

superlative Many adjectives have three different forms. These are known as the positive, the comparative, and the superlative. The comparative and superlative are used when you make comparisons.

The positive form of an adjective is given as the entry in the dictionary. It is used when there is no comparison between different objects:
Dekel is *tall*.

The superlative form is usually made by adding the ending *-est* to the positive form of the adjective. It shows that something possesses a quality to a greater extent than all the others in its class or group:

Dekel is the *tallest* boy in his class.

You can also express superlatives by using the words *most* or *least* with the positive (not the superlative) form of the adjective:
Dekel is the *most energetic* member of the family.

symbolism Used to express abstract ideas through the symbolic use of images.

T

techno- The prefix that is used at the beginning of words that refer to technology. For example, if you refer to someone as a *technophobe*, you mean that they do not like new technology, such as computers or mobile telephones, and are afraid to use it.

tense There are twelve different tenses. First, are those straightforward expressions to indicate present, past and future intention:

Present *I go to the city once a week.*

Past *I went to the city last week.*

Future *I will go to the city next week.*

However, when we need to express continuing action in these three tenses we have to use the progressive forms:

Present progressive *I am going to the city to see Simon.*

Past progressive *I was going to the city but Simon cancelled.*

Future progressive *I will be going to the city again next week.*

The next set of tenses allows us to qualify the basic past and future tenses. If, for example, we use the past tense to say *I went to the city*, we are referring to an action that took place some time before the present; perhaps I went to the city last week, yesterday, or an hour ago, but since then I have returned. The action is over. But what if we need to convey the impression that *I've gone to the city but haven't returned*? What we need here is a tense that indicates not only past action, but past action that continues or could continue right up to the present moment.

Present perfect *I have gone to the city and will be back tonight.*

Past perfect *I had gone to the city without my briefcase.*

Future perfect *I will have gone to the city by the time you get to my flat.*

You will see that the present perfect tense indicates that while I have gone to the city I am still there – in other words, the action that began in the past is extended to the present moment. The past perfect tense indicates that a past action had taken place (my going to the city) at an earlier time than another action (discovering that I'd forgotten my briefcase). The future perfect tense indicates that a future action (my going to the city) is likely to take place at an earlier time than another future action (your getting to my flat).

-th A prefix that is added to written numbers ending in 4, 5, 6, 7, 8, 9, 10, 11, 12 or 13 in order to form ordinal numbers, for example, *14th February is Valentine's Day.*

that A relative pronoun that replaces a noun which links two different parts of a sentence.
We could go to a place *that* I know.

That refers to things or people. It is never used immediately after a preposition, but it can be used if the preposition is separated from the relative pronoun:
It was a film *that* I had little interest *in.*

the The definite article that is used before a noun to refer to a specific example of that noun:
the kitchen table
the school I attend

The definite article *the* may be used before singular and plural nouns. However, you cannot use the indefinite article *a* or *an* before a plural noun. You need to use the word *some* in this case:
the tables → *some* tables
the schools → *some* schools

third person see person.

trans- A prefix that is used to form adjectives which indicate that something moves or enables travel from one side of an area to another. For example, a *blood transfusion* is a process in which blood is injected into the body of a person who is badly injured or ill.

transitive verb A verb which takes an object: She's *wasting* her *money.*

tri- A prefix that forms nouns and adjectives which have *three* as part of their meaning. For example, a *tricycle* is a cycle with three wheels.

U

ultra- A prefix that forms adjectives which refer to people and things that possess a quality to a very large degree. For example, an ultra-light fabric is extremely light.

un- A prefix that can be added to some words to form words which have the opposite meaning. For example, if something is *unacceptable*, it is not acceptable.

uncount noun A noun which has only one form, takes a singular verb, and is not used with a or numbers. Uncount nouns often refer to substances, qualities, feelings, activities, and abstract ideas: *coal, courage, anger, help, fun.*

under- A prefix that forms words which refer to an amount or value being too low or not enough. For example, if someone is *underweight*, their weight is lower than it should be.

V

verb A verb is a word that describes an action or a state of being. Verbs are sometimes called "doing words".

Verbs of state indicate the way things are:
Robert *is* a Taurus.
Anna *has* one sister.

Verbs of action indicate specific events that happen, have happened or will happen:
Purvisha *visits* the dentist.
The man *faxed* his order.

Auxiliary verbs are used in combination with other verbs to allow the user to distinguish between different times, different degrees of completion, and different amounts of certainty:
Purvisha *will* visit the dentist.
The man *is* faxing his order.
They *may* talk for up to three hours.

Phrasal verbs consist of a verb followed by either an adverb or a preposition. The two words taken together have a special meaning which could not be deduced from their literal meanings:
The car *broke down* again.
When did you *take up* croquet?

Impersonal verbs are verbs that do not have a subject and are only used after *it* or *there*:
It *rains* here every day.

Modal Verbs are usually used as auxiliary verbs to change the tone of the meaning of another verb. They include, *can, could, may, might, must, should, would,* and *ought*:
I wonder if you can come.
Even when they are used on their own, they suggest another verb:
I certainly can. (i.e. I certainly can come)

There is no difference between the third person present and the other forms of the present tense. No form of the verb ends in -*s*:
I can speak German.
She can speak German.

These verbs do not have a present participle or a past participle.
The verb *could* may be used as the past tense of can:
I could speak German when I was younger.

You can talk about past time by using *could have, may have, might have, must have, should have, would have,* and *ought to have*:
We may have taken a wrong turning.
She must have thought I was stupid.

verb group A main verb, or a main verb with one or more auxiliaries, a modal, or a modal and an auxiliary, which is used with a subject to say what someone does, or what happens to them:
I'll show them.
She's been ill.

vice- A prefix that is used before a rank or title to indicate that someone is next in importance to the person who holds the rank or title mentioned. For example, a *vice-president* is next in importance to the president.

wh- question A question which expects the answer to give more information than just *yes* or *no*:
What happened?
Where did he go?

wh- word One of a group of words starting with *wh-*, such as *what*, *when* or *who*, which are used in *wh-* questions. *How* is also called a *wh-* word because it behaves like the other *wh-* words.

which A relative pronoun that replaces a noun which links two different parts of a sentence. *Which* is only used when the antecedent is not a person:
We took the road which leads to the sea.

who A relative pronoun that replaces a noun which links two different parts of a sentence. The forms *who, whom,* and *whose* are used when the antecedent is a person. *Who* indicates the subject of the verb:
It was the same person who saw me yesterday.
It was the person whom I saw yesterday.

The distinction between *who* and *whom* is often ignored in everyday English, and *who* is often used as the object:
It was the person who I saw yesterday.

whom A relative pronoun that replaces a noun which links two different parts of a sentence. The forms *who, whom,* and *whose* are used when the antecedent is a person. *Whom* indicates the object of the verb:
It was the same person who saw me yesterday.
It was the person whom I saw yesterday.

The distinction between *who* and *whom* is often ignored in everyday English, and *who* is often used as the object:
It was the person who I saw yesterday.

Whom is used immediately after a preposition. However, if the preposition is separated from the relative pronoun, *who* is usually used:
He is a man in whom I have great confidence.
He is a man who I have great confidence in.

whose A relative pronoun that replaces a noun which links two different parts of a sentence. The forms *who*, *whom*, and *whose* are used when the antecedent is a person. *Whose* is the possessive form of the relative pronoun. It can refer to things as well as people:
Anna has a sister whose name is Rosie.
I found a book whose pages were torn.

will The verbs *will* and *shall* have only one form. They do not have a present form ending in -s, and they do not have a present participle, a past tense, or a past participle. These verbs are used as auxiliary verbs to form the future tense:
She will give a talk about Chinese history.
We shall arrive on Thursday.

People used to use *shall* to indicate the first person, and *will* to indicate the second person and the third person. However, this distinction is often ignored now:
I will see you on Sunday.
I shall see you on Sunday.

Shall is always used in questions involving *I* and *we*. *Will* is avoided in these cases:
Shall I put the cat out?
Shall we dance?

Will is always used when making polite requests, giving orders, and indicating persistence. *Shall* is avoided in these cases:
Will you please help me?
Will you be quiet!
She will keep going on about Al Pacino.

Y

-y A suffix that forms adjectives which indicate that something is full of something else or covered in it. For example, if something is *dirty*, it is covered with dirt. It also forms adjectives which mean that something is like something else. For example, if something tastes *chocolatey*, it tastes like chocolate, although it is not actually chocolate.

yes/no -question A question which can be answered by just *yes* or *no,* without giving any more information:
Would you like some more tea?